DOGS AT WORK

SEARCH AND RESCUE DOGS

BY MATT LILLEY

WWW.APEXEDITIONS.COM

Copyright © 2023 by Apex Editions, Mendota Heights, MN 55120. All rights reserved. No part of this book may be reproduced or utilized in any form or by any means without written permission from the publisher.

Apex is distributed by North Star Editions:
sales@northstareditions.com | 888-417-0195

Produced for Apex by Red Line Editorial.

Photographs ©: Shutterstock Images, cover, 1, 4–5, 6–7, 8–9, 10–11, 12–13, 14, 15, 16–17, 18, 20, 21, 22–23, 24–25, 26–27, 29

Library of Congress Control Number: 2022912281

ISBN
978-1-63738-424-4 (hardcover)
978-1-63738-451-0 (paperback)
978-1-63738-504-3 (ebook pdf)
978-1-63738-478-7 (hosted ebook)

Printed in the United States of America
Mankato, MN
012023

NOTE TO PARENTS AND EDUCATORS

Apex books are designed to build literacy skills in striving readers. Exciting, high-interest content attracts and holds readers' attention. The text is carefully leveled to allow students to achieve success quickly. Additional features, such as bolded glossary words for difficult terms, help build comprehension.

TABLE OF CONTENTS

CHAPTER 1
LOST AND FOUND 4

CHAPTER 2
MANY JOBS 10

CHAPTER 3
DIFFERENT SKILLS 16

CHAPTER 4
TRAINING 22

COMPREHENSION QUESTIONS • 28
GLOSSARY • 30
TO LEARN MORE • 31
ABOUT THE AUTHOR • 31
INDEX • 32

CHAPTER 1

LOST AND FOUND

A little girl is lost in the woods. The police bring in a search and rescue (SAR) dog to help. The dog sniffs the girl's pillow. He learns her scent.

A dog's sense of smell is more than 1,000 times better than a human's.

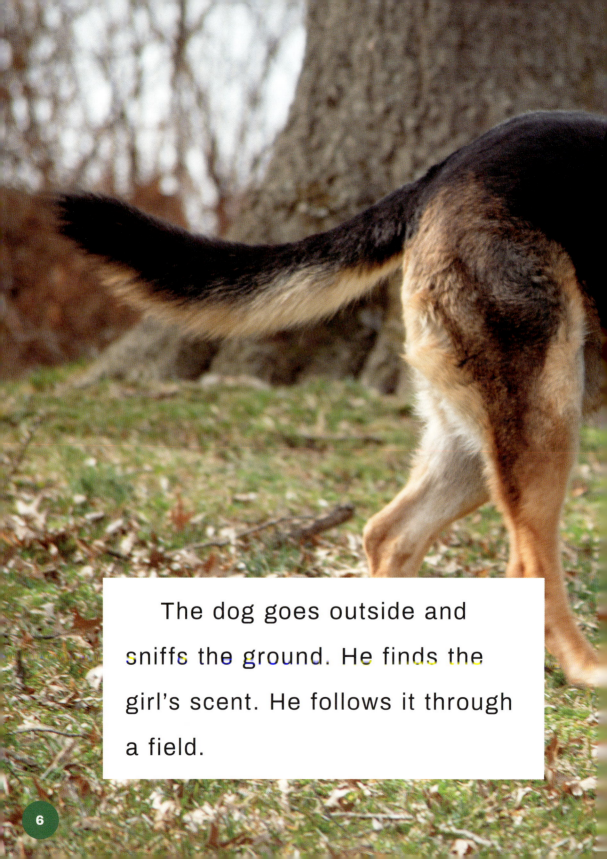

The dog goes outside and sniffs the ground. He finds the girl's scent. He follows it through a field.

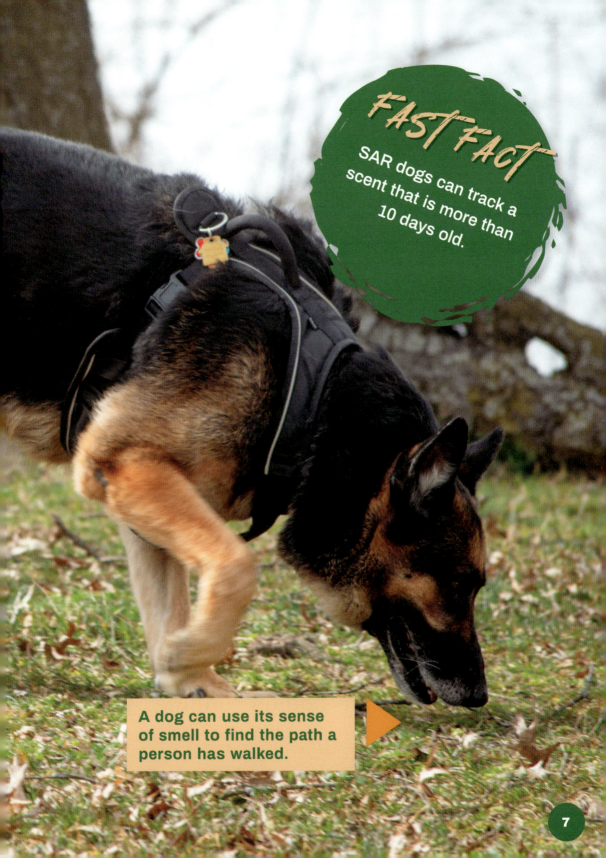

FAST FACT SAR dogs can track a scent that is more than 10 days old.

A dog can use its sense of smell to find the path a person has walked.

7

The dog finds the girl. He barks to alert his **handler**. The rescue team comes running. The girl is safe.

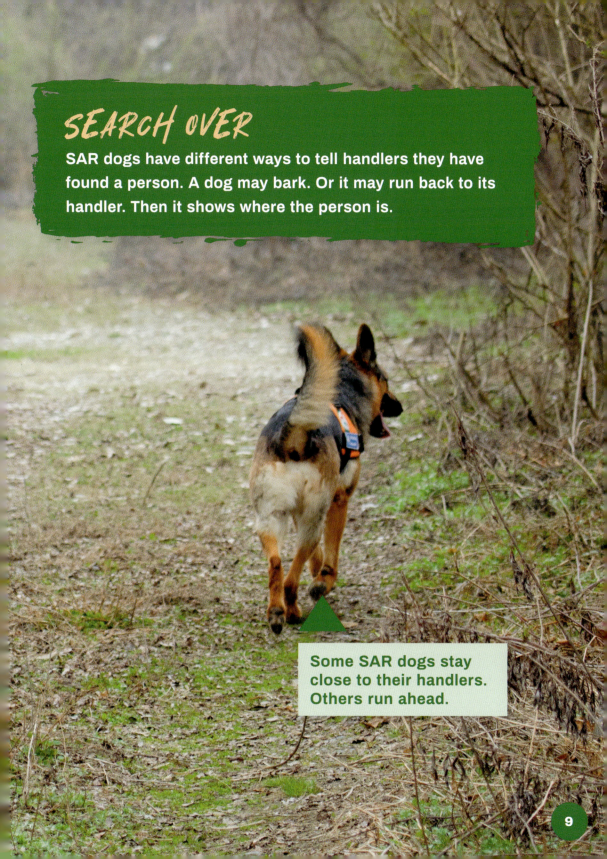

SEARCH OVER

SAR dogs have different ways to tell handlers they have found a person. A dog may bark. Or it may run back to its handler. Then it shows where the person is.

Some SAR dogs stay close to their handlers. Others run ahead.

CHAPTER 2

MANY JOBS

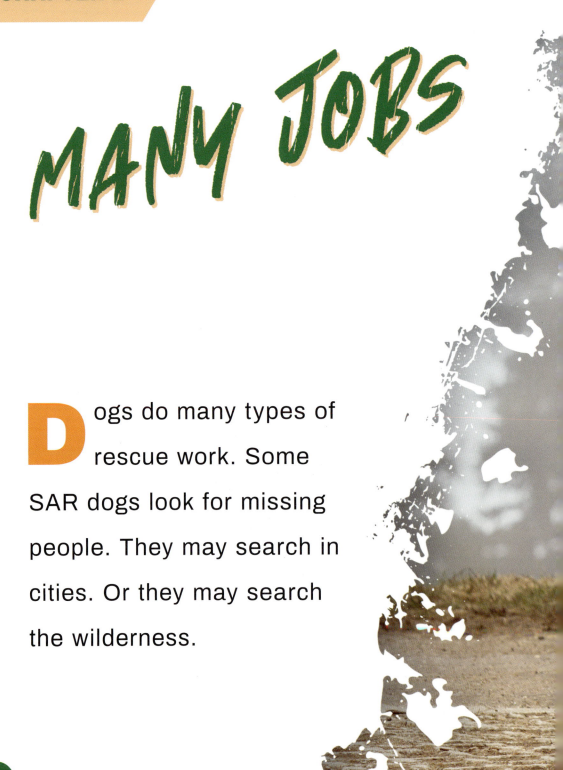

Dogs do many types of rescue work. Some SAR dogs look for missing people. They may search in cities. Or they may search the wilderness.

SAR dogs often help find hikers who are lost in the woods.

Other dogs work in disaster areas. Buildings can collapse in earthquakes or storms. Dogs search the **rubble** for **survivors**.

Disaster dogs find people who are hurt or trapped.

FAST FACT

SAR dogs must work quickly. People found sooner have a better chance of surviving.

Avalanche dogs often work on cold, snowy mountains.

Some SAR dogs do water rescues. They save people from drowning. Other dogs help after **avalanches**. They find people who are buried under snow.

Newfoundlands are trained to do rescues on beaches or boats.

WATER DOGS

Newfoundlands often work as water rescue dogs. Newfies are large and strong. And they are great swimmers. They can pull ropes or floats to help people swim.

CHAPTER 3

DIFFERENT SKILLS

Depending on their jobs, SAR dogs follow scents in different ways. Tracking and trailing dogs follow the scent of one particular person.

To a dog, each person's skin has a different smell.

These dogs start from the person's last known location. They smell something the person touched. Then they follow the scent along the ground.

FAST FACT
Most SAR dogs and their handlers are volunteers. They do not get paid for their work.

◀ **Bloodhounds are good at trailing scents on the ground.**

Disaster dogs are usually air-scenting dogs.

Air-scenting dogs search for the smells of any nearby people. First, dogs sniff the air. Then, they find a scent's source. These dogs often search big areas.

DIFFERENT BREEDS

All dogs have good senses of smell. But some breeds can smell better than others. German shepherds make great air-scenting dogs. So do Labrador retrievers.

Saint Bernard dogs became famous for saving people on snowy mountains.

CHAPTER 4

TRAINING

Search and rescue teams must be officially **certified**. Dogs and their handlers must pass tests. To build their skills, they practice and train.

During training, people hide so dogs can practice finding them.

Training a dog can be like hide-and-seek. A person hides with the dog's toy. When the dog finds the person, they play with the toy. This reward helps **motivate** the dog.

FAST FACT

Handlers go through training, too. They learn about giving help and surviving in the wild.

24

Some SAR dogs begin training when they are just 8 to 10 weeks old.

After being certified, dogs and handlers continue training. That way, their skills stay fresh.

It takes about 600 hours to fully train an SAR dog.

THE RIGHT AGE

Most SAR dogs are between two and five years old. These dogs are old enough to have experience. But they are still young enough to be very athletic.

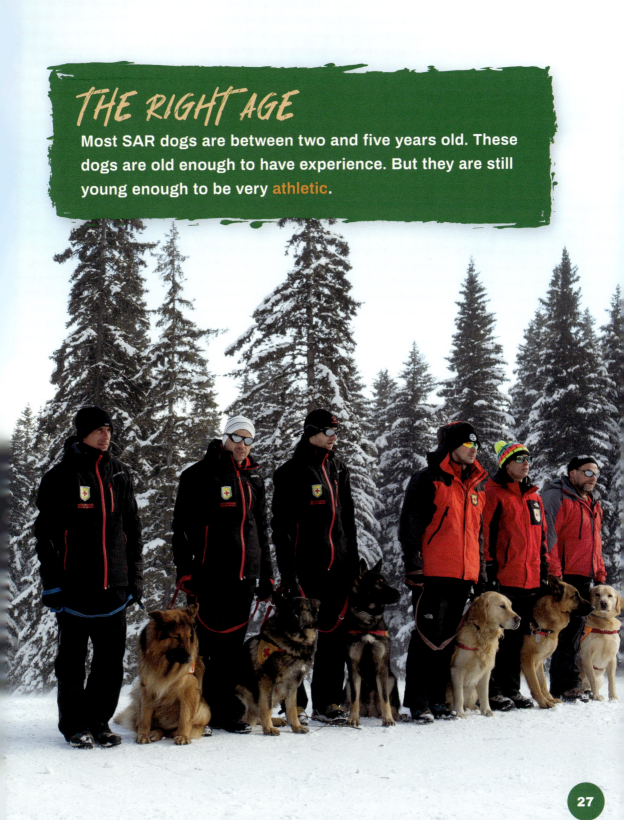

COMPREHENSION QUESTIONS

Write your answers on a separate piece of paper.

1. Write a paragraph that explains the main ideas of Chapter 3.

2. If you could train a search and rescue dog, what type would you choose? Why?

3. Which type of dog follows a scent along the ground?
   - A. tracking dog
   - B. air-scenting dog
   - C. water rescue dog

4. Which type of dog could help search for many people in a large area?
   - A. tracking dog
   - B. trailing dog
   - C. air-scenting dog

5. What does **volunteers** mean in this book?

Most SAR dogs and their handlers are volunteers. They do not get paid for their work.

    A. workers who make lots of money
    B. workers who do tasks for free
    C. animals that live in zoos

6. What does **fresh** mean in this book?

After being certified, dogs and handlers continue training. That way, their skills stay fresh.

    A. newly picked
    B. newly cleaned
    C. ready to use

Answer key on page 32.

GLOSSARY

athletic
Showing speed, strength, or other active skills.

avalanches
Times when lots of snow falls quickly down the side of a mountain.

breeds
Specific types of dogs that have their own looks and abilities.

certified
Proved to have certain skills and training, often by passing a test.

handler
A person who works with and trains an animal.

motivate
To get someone to do or repeat an action.

rubble
Pieces of buildings that have fallen apart.

survivors
People who stayed alive during a time of danger.

BOOKS

Davidson, B. Keith. *Search and Rescue Dog*. New York: Crabtree Branches, 2022.

Markle, Sandra. *Animals to the Rescue!: Amazing True Stories from Around the World*. Minneapolis: Millbrook Press, 2022.

Pearson, Marie. *Dog Trainer*. North Mankato, MN: Capstone Press, 2019.

ONLINE RESOURCES

Visit www.apexeditions.com to find links and resources related to this title.

ABOUT THE AUTHOR

Matt Lilley has an MS in scientific and technical writing. The focus of his degree was on medical writing for kids. He loves researching and writing about all sorts of topics. He lives in Minnesota with his family.

INDEX

A
air-scenting dogs, 20–21
avalanches, 14

E
earthquakes, 12

G
German shepherds, 21

H
handlers, 8–9, 19, 22, 24, 26

L
Labrador retrievers, 21

N
Newfoundlands, 15

P
police, 4

S
scent, 4, 6–7, 16, 19–20
skills, 22, 26
smell, 19–21
snow, 14
storms, 12

T
tracking dogs, 7, 16, 19
trailing dogs, 16, 19
training, 22, 24, 26

V
volunteers, 19

W
water, 14–15

ANSWER KEY:
1. Answers will vary; 2. Answers will vary; 3. A; 4. C; 5. B; 6. C